Copyright © 2025 Jennifer Jones
All copyright laws and rights reserved.
Published in the U.S.A.
For more information, email info@ninjalifehacks.tv
Paperback ISBN: 978-1-63731-963-5
Hardcover ISBN: 978-1-63731-965-9
eBook ISBN: 978-1-63731-964-2

Find the Pumpkins on Strike lesson plans at ninjalifehacks.tv

They'd been poked, sliced and painted up,
and filled with gooey guts.
Some were dropped or kicked around.
Those Halloween kids were nuts!

Then something odd began to spread from porches to the patch. The pumpkins all had vanished, not one was left to catch!

The Pumpkin Union

You draw weird faces on our skin,

then throw us out in rain.

We'd like to feel important too,

not tossed beside a drain.

Now every fall they still carve fun,
but treat each one with care.
They name them, thank them, light them up,
then keep them safe somewhere.

So if your pumpkins disappear
or run away one night,
just try a little kindness,
and you might make things right!

Design Your Own Pumpkin Pal!

Give your pumpkin a name, outfit, and superpower!

My pumpkin's name: _____
What they wear: _____
_____
Superpower: _____

Draw your pumpkin here!